Jewish
holy days

Lisa Magloff

Lighting candles for Chanukkah.

Glossary

ABRAHAM One of the founders, or fathers, of Judaism. He was the first person to make an agreement with God. Abraham promised God that he would worship only God, and in exchange, God promised to make Abraham the 'father' of a great nation.

ARK This is the cabinet in which the Torah scrolls are kept in the synagogue. The word Ark is a shorter way of saying the Hebrew name of the cabinet: Aron Kodesh.

HEBREW The language spoken by the ancient Jews and the language of modern Israel. Jewish people are sometimes referred to as Hebrews or Hebrew people.

HIGH HOLY DAYS The days between Rosh Hashanah and Yom Kippur. Traditionally, these days are thought to be the time when God decides everyone's fate for the coming year.

ISRAELITE/ISRAELI The descendents of Abraham were called Israelites (from the name Israel, the name God gave to Abraham's grandson Jacob).

JEW A person who follows the Jewish faith, or any person whose mother was a Jew or who converted to Judaism. The word 'Jew' (in Hebrew, *Yehudi*) comes from the name Judah, which was the name of one of Jacob's 12 sons. Originally, the term Jew referred only to members of the tribe of Judah. However, the nation of Israel was split into two kingdoms – Judea and Israel – and all the people of Israel were taken into captivity in Babylon. The people of Judea were left behind, so after this time the Israelites were all referred to as Jews.

JUDAISM The religion of the Jewish people.

MENORAH A candelabrum. It usually refers to a seven or nine-branched candelabrum in the synagogue, or an eight-branched candelabrum used during Chanukkah.

REPENTANCE To feel sorry for something bad you have done. When you try to make up for the bad thing, that is called atonement.

SHABBAT The Jewish day of rest. It runs from sundown on Friday to sundown Saturday.

SHOFAR A ram's horn, blown like a trumpet as a call to repentance on Rosh Hashanah.

SYNAGOGUE The Jewish house of worship.

TEMPLE The central place of worship in ancient Jerusalem, where prayers and animal sacrifices were offered to God. The Temple was destroyed twice in ancient times, the last time by the Romans in 129 CE. After this it was never rebuilt. The Western Wall of the Temple, in Jerusalem, is the only part of the ancient building that can still be seen and is considered a holy site for Jews.

TEN PLAGUES To convince the Pharaoh to let the Hebrew slaves leave Egypt, God sent ten plagues to Egypt: blood, frogs, lice, flies, cattle disease, boils, hail, locusts, darkness, and the death of all the Egyptian first-born.

TORAH The Jewish Bible. The word Torah refers to both the first five books of the Bible, sometimes called the Books of Moses, or the Pentateuch, and to the entire body of Jewish teachings.

Contents

As you go through the book, look for words in **BOLD CAPITALS**. These words are defined in the glossary.

 Understanding others

Remember that other people's beliefs are important to them. You must always be considerate and understanding when studying about faith.

A menorah for Chanukkah.

What is a holy day?

As in other faiths, Jewish holidays celebrate important events in the year.

People of all faiths worship throughout the whole year. But in all faiths, some days are special. These special days, or holy days, may remember an important event in the history of the faith, or they may be written about in holy writings, or scripture.

These holy days are different from a day of rest and worship that many religions have each week. Many holy days involve public celebrations, special meals, festivals and even processions. In general, we call these special days holy days and it is from this that we get the word 'holiday'.

▼ These children are visiting the Western Wall of the ancient TEMPLE in Jerusalem, one of the most important sites in JUDAISM.

▶ Many holy days are celebrated at home, with special meals, prayers and readings.

In the Jewish faith, the weekly day of rest is called **SHABBAT** (this is the **HEBREW** word for Sabbath). Shabbat begins at sundown on Friday night and lasts until sundown on Saturday. But there are many holy days throughout the year, each with their own name.

As you look at the main holy days of the Jewish faith, notice how each day is marked out or celebrated in a different way. Some holy days remember difficult times in the past and are solemn days of prayer. Others are happy and joyous celebrations. Most Jewish holidays involve worship in the **SYNAGOGUE** and at home.

◀ This woman is wearing fancy dress to celebrate the holiday of Purim.

5

The Jewish holy day calendar

Here are the parts of the year when Jewish holidays occur. The actual date varies from one year to another.

Today, many people in the world use a calendar which divides the year into 12 months and begins on January 1. In this calendar, the Sun is used as a guide and one year is about the time it takes the Earth to move around the Sun. But not all calendars look like this. Some calendars, for example, use the way the Moon moves across the sky as a guide. This is how the Jewish people organised their calendar, thousands of years ago.

In the Jewish calendar, each month has 29 or 30 days and a thirteenth month is added in leap years, every two or three years.

Dates

Dates are give as BCE, which means Before Common Era, and CE, which means Common Era. These are the same as the Christian BC and AD, but have no direct religious connection.

In this chart, you can see how the Jewish holy days are spread around the year. You can also see how the days move around a little from year to year.

▲ Many people visit the Western Wall during holy days to pray.

Jewish months	
Nissan	March/April
Iyar	April/May
Sivan	May/June
Tammuz	June/July
Av	July/August
Elul	August/September
Tishri	September/October
Cheshvan	October/November
Kislev	November/December
Tevet	December/January
Shevat	January/February
Adar I	February/March (leap years only)
Adar	February/March (called Adar II in leap years)

JEWISH HOLY DAYS

	2007	2008	2009	2010	2011
Rosh Hashanah	Sept 13	Sept 30	Sept 19	Sept 9	Sept 29
Yom Kippur	Sept 22	Oct 9	Sept 28	Sept 18	Oct 8
Sukkot	Sept 27	Oct 14	Oct 3	Sept 23	Oct 13
Chanukkah	Dec 5	Dec 22	Dec 12	Dec 2	Dec 21
Purim	March 4	March 21	March 10	Feb 28	March 20
Pesach	April 3	April 20	April 9	March 30	April 19
Shavuot	May 22	June 9	May 29	May 19	June 8

All holidays begin at sundown on the day before the date given here.

Rosh Hashanah – New Year

This holiday celebrates the Jewish New Year.

The Jewish year begins with a holy day – the New Year (on the common calendar this falls in September or October).

The New Year holiday celebrates two things. It celebrates the start of a new year; and it also celebrates the day that Jewish tradition says that God created Adam, the first human.

So, Rosh Hashanah is the time to celebrate God's creation of the world and everything in it. This is a happy time, and a time to wish for a good future and good fortune for everyone.

▼ A horn called a shofar, made from a ram's horn, is blown during worship on Rosh Hashanah.

During Rosh Hashanah, people greet each other with the Hebrew words, "*L'shanah tovah*", which mean 'For a good year'.

Celebrating Rosh Hashanah in the synagogue

In the synagogue, there is a long worship service. During the service, the TORAH is taken out of its cabinet and read aloud. There are also special prayers and songs, which are used only on this day.

A special feature of this service is the blowing of a ram's horn. It makes a sound like a deep trumpet. This ram's horn trumpet is called a SHOFAR. In ancient Israel, the shofar was blown during the coronation (crowning ceremony) of kings, so it is a reminder that God is King. During worship services around 100 shofar blasts are sounded.

◀ The Torah being taken out from the ARK.

Judaism actually has several different 'New Years'. One Jewish New Year starts in September/October, with the month of Tishri. This is the New Year for years, the time when the year number increases.

However, the first month on the Jewish calendar is Nissan, which occurs in March/April. Nissan 1 is the New Year for the purpose of counting the reign of ancient kings and months on the calendar. There are other New Years as well, such as Shevat 15 (in February), which is the New Year for counting the age of trees.

All of this may seem a bit odd, but you can think of it as similar to the way the 'New Year' on the common calendar starts in January, but the new 'school year', which is the new year for counting school years, starts in September.

Weblink: www.CurriculumVisions.com

▼ In some traditions, on Rosh Hashanah, round foods like these doughnuts, are eaten as a reminder of the cycle of the seasons of the year.

Celebrating Rosh Hashanah at home

Like many other parts of Jewish life, celebration at home is as important as celebrating in the synagogue. There are many ways that people celebrate Rosh Hashanah at home.

One Rosh Hashanah tradition is to eat sweet foods, such as slices of apple dipped in honey, with family and friends. This is a way to show that we hope everyone's New Year will be sweet and full of good things.

▲ One Rosh Hashanah tradition is to eat apples dipped in honey. This shows the hope that the New Year will be 'sweet'.

Another Rosh Hashanah tradition is called casting off, or tashlich. People put breadcrumbs in their pockets and then go to a lake or river and throw the breadcrumbs in the water. The breadcrumbs stand for anything bad that can happen. So, throwing the breadcrumbs in the water is another way to show that people are hoping for a good year.

◀ In some Jewish traditions, people eat a whole, cooked fish on Rosh Hashanah. There are many reasons for this. One is that the fish stands for the hope of a prosperous New Year. Just like there are many fish in the sea, people hope to have many good things happen in the New Year.

On Rosh Hashanah, the head of the fish might be placed before the head of the family. He or she then says: "May it be God's will that we be like the head (leaders) and not like the tail (followers)."

Weblink: www.CurriculumVisions.com

The Days of Awe

Rosh Hashanah is also the first day of a holy period of ten days. This period is called the **HIGH HOLY DAYS** or the Days of Awe.

Jewish tradition says that on Rosh Hashanah, God opens a big book called the Book of Life. During the next ten days, God will write down in the book everything that will happen to us during the next year. After ten days, on a holy day called Yom Kippur (see pages 14 to 17), God shuts the book. So, the ten days in-between Rosh Hashanah and Yom Kippur are a time for Jewish people to show God that they deserve to have a good year.

How do people try to persuade God to give them a good year? One way is through prayer. Another is by doing good deeds and helping others. One of the most important ways is by feeling sorry for any bad things they have done in the past year. For example, many people try to apologise to anyone they may have hurt during the past year. They may also apologise to God through prayer.

Trying to make up for any bad things you have done is called **REPENTANCE**, and you will find it in most religions.

▼ Worshippers in Jerusalem pray during the Days of Awe next to the Western Wall, the only part of the ancient Temple that still exists.

Yom Kippur – sealing the Book of Life

Yom Kippur marks the end of the ten Days of Awe.

Yom Kippur occurs ten days after Rosh Hashanah (September or October in the common calendar). It marks the end of the Days of Awe.

In Jewish tradition, Yom Kippur is the day on which God seals the Book of Life. On this day, God makes the final decision on what will happen to each person in the New Year.

The name 'Yom Kippur' also means 'Day of Atonement'. Atonement means 'to make up for'; so this is the last day when Jewish people can make up for any bad things they have done and show God that they deserve to have a good year.

Fasting

One way that people show God they are sorry for any bad things they may have done is by fasting (not eating). So, on Yom Kippur, many people do not eat or drink anything for 25 hours.

> The Lord said to Moses, "The tenth day of this seventh month is the Day of Atonement.
>
> Hold a sacred assembly and deny yourselves, and present an offering made to the LORD by fire.
>
> Do no work on that day, because it is the Day of Atonement, when atonement is made for you before the LORD your God."
>
> *(Leviticus 23:26–28)*

In the synagogue

Many **JEWS** spend most of Yom Kippur praying in the synagogue. Worship services on Yom Kippur are much longer than on any other holy day and include many special prayers asking for God's forgiveness.

Remember that Jewish holy days begin at sunset and go on to the following sunset. So, on Yom Kippur, the first worship service begins just after sunset. This service starts with a prayer called the kol nidre, or 'all vows'. In this prayer, Jewish people ask God to cancel any promises they might make to God during the year that they are not able to keep.

This prayer is made because, throughout history, there have been many times when Jewish people were forced to make promises they could not keep.

For example, during the Middle Ages in Europe, the Roman Catholic Inquisition in some countries tortured some Jews until they promised to convert to Christianity. Even though they made the promise against their will, they felt that they had to keep the promise unless God released them from it. The kol nidre prayer on Yom Kippur was designed to do this.

The next morning, there is a special memorial service (called Yizkor) for loved ones who have died.

During the final worship service of Yom Kippur the **ARK** (the cabinet where the Torah scrolls are kept) is left open, and so everyone must stand throughout the entire service.

This service is sometimes called 'the closing of the gates' because it is a 'last chance' before the holy day ends to repent and make up to God for anything bad that a person may have done. The service ends with a very long blast of the shofar.

After the last worship service, people gather together for a meal to break the 25-hour fast.

The kol nidre prayer

"All vows, obligations, oaths or anathemas, pledges of all names, which we have vowed, sworn, devoted, or bound ourselves to, from this day of atonement, until the next day of atonement (whose arrival we hope for in happiness) we repent, aforehand, of them all, they shall all be deemed absolved, forgiven, annulled, void and made of no effect; they shall not be binding, nor have any power; the vows shall not be reckoned as vows, the obligations shall not be obligatory, nor the oaths considered as oaths."

A Yom Kippur story

On some Jewish holy days, certain parts of the Torah (Jewish Bible) are read out loud in the synagogue. On Yom Kippur, the story of Jonah and the whale from the Torah Book of Jonah is often read out loud in the synagogue.

The story begins when God asks Jonah to preach against evil. But Jonah is afraid to do what God asked and he runs away to sea.

At sea, God sends a terrible wind that threatens the ship. Jonah knew that God sent the storm because he had disobeyed God, so Jonah asks the sailors to throw him overboard.

The sailors throw Jonah overboard, where he is swallowed up by a whale. Inside the whale, Jonah asks for God's forgiveness and so God causes the whale to vomit him onto dry land.

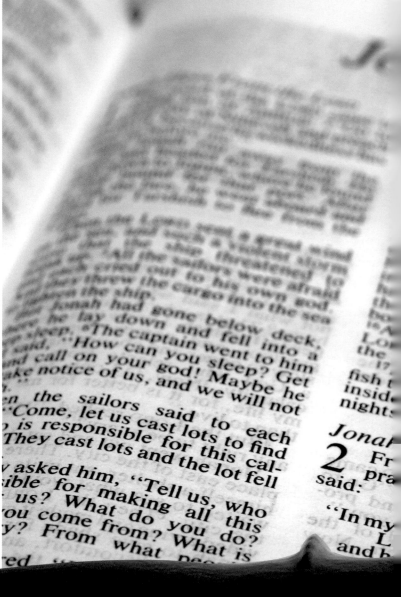

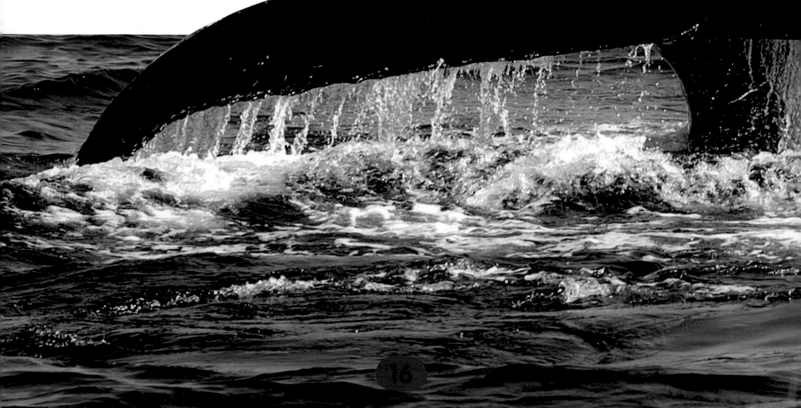

Finally, Jonah does what God told him to do. He travels to a city called Ninevah and tells the people there that God is angry with them because they are wicked, and that in 40 days the city will be destroyed. When the people of Ninevah hear this they become very scared. They fast and repent for all the bad things they have done and pray to God to forgive them. So, God forgives them and does not destroy the city.

Unfortunately, Jonah has still not learned to trust God and he is angry at God's decision, because he thinks that wicked people should be punished. Then God tells him:

"Ninevah has more than a hundred and twenty thousand people who cannot tell their right hand from their left, and many cattle as well. Should I not be concerned about that great city?"

The lesson of the story is the lesson of Yom Kippur. God wants people to be good, but God knows it is hard to be good all the time. But if people are truly sorry for anything bad they have done, then God will forgive them.

Chanukkah

Chanukkah celebrates an important historical event and a miracle.

Chanukkah is an eight day festival that begins on the 25th day of the Jewish month of Kislev (November/December).

Chanukkah celebrates an historical event, when a small group of Jews defeated the mighty Assyrian army in ancient times.

▼ An eight-branched candelabra called a MENORAH is used to celebrate Chanukkah. The ninth candle is used to light the other eight.

The story of Chanukkah

More than 2,100 years ago, an Assyrian king ruled over the land of Israel. He outlawed the practice of the Jewish religion, and he put statues of Greek gods inside the Jewish sacred Temple in Jerusalem.

Some Jews gave up their religion and began worshipping the Greek gods, but other Jews rebelled against the new laws. The most successful rebel was a priest named Mattathias. Mattathias and his five sons formed an army. They called themselves the Maccabees, which means 'hammer'. After three years, the Maccabees defeated the Assyrians and drove them out of Israel.

After their victory, the Jewish priests took the Greek statues out of the Temple and wanted to rededicate the Temple to God. To do this they needed sacred oil to relight the sacred lamp in the Temple. This lamp was supposed to always be kept burning.

But most of the sacred oil had been destroyed by the Assyrians and it would take eight days to make more oil. There was only enough sacred oil left to burn for one day. But when the oil was poured into the lamp, it burned for eight days. This is the miracle of Chanukkah.

19

Chanukkah customs

At Chanukkah Jewish people remember the miracle of the oil, and the fight for freedom, by lighting candles at home while saying blessings to God.

Each night at home, a new candle is lit on the menorah (a candlestick which holds eight candles). The candles are lit with a ninth candle called a helper candle.

In some Jewish traditions, foods which have been fried in oil, like potato pancakes, are eaten during the eight days of Chanukkah. These are another reminder of the miracle of the oil.

During Chanukkah children might also play a game with a four-sided spinning top. This game may have come from the time when the Assyrians outlawed the study of the Jewish holy books. Many Jews continued to study in secret, and in order to hide what they were really doing, they would keep a spinning top nearby. If they were found by the Assyrian troops, they would pretend they were just playing a game.

In modern times, some Jewish communities have started the custom of giving gifts to children on Chanukkah. One popular gift is chocolate coins.

▲ Chocolate coins wrapped in gold-coloured foil are a popular and tasty modern Chanukkah treat.

▲ Fried foods like these potato pancakes are eaten on Chanukkah as a reminder of the miracle of the oil.

◀ Each night a new candle is lit on the menorah until, on the last night, all eight candles are lit up.

▲ This boy is playing a Chanukkah game with a spinning top called a dreidle.

Weblink: www.CurriculumVisions.com

Pesach – Passover

This spring festival remembers the exodus from Egypt and the suffering of slavery.

The festival of Passover (called Pesach in Hebrew) always begins on the 15th day of the Jewish month of Nissan, at the beginning of springtime, and lasts for seven days.

Pesach remembers a time when God helped the ancestors of the Jewish people to escape from slavery in Egypt and, after 40 years of wandering in the desert, brought them to the promised land that would become Israel. The story is told in the Torah book of Exodus.

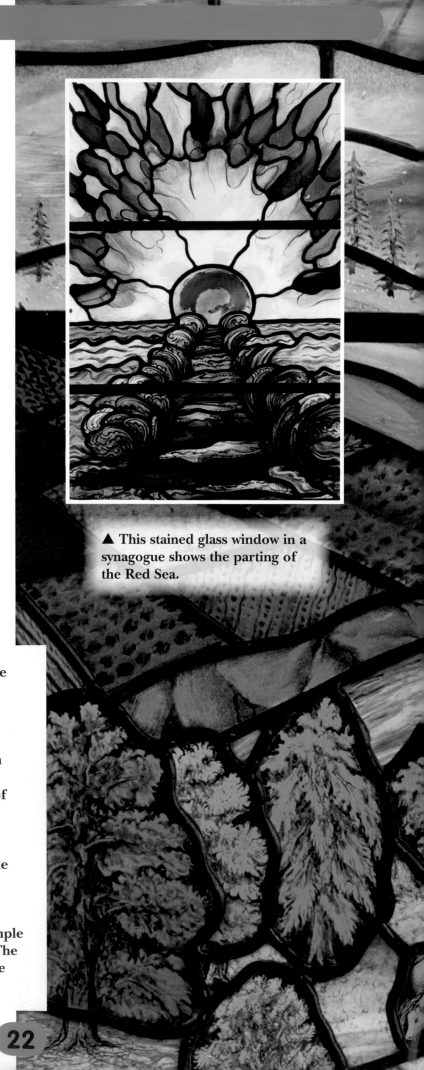

▲ This stained glass window in a synagogue shows the parting of the Red Sea.

In the Exodus story in the Torah, the Jewish people were not actually called 'Jews'. In the Torah, the descendents of ABRAHAM were called ISRAELITES (from the name Israel, the name God gave to Abraham's grandson Jacob).

The word 'Jew' (in Hebrew, *Yehudi*) comes from the name Judah, which was the name of one of Jacob's 12 sons. Judah founded one of the tribes of Israel, which was named after him. Originally, the term Jew referred only to members of the tribe of Judah. However, after the death of King Solomon, the nation of Israel was split into two kingdoms: the kingdom of Judah (called Judea) and the kingdom of Israel.

In 587 BCE, the Assyrian king Nebuchadnezzer captured the kingdom of Israel, destroyed the Temple and took all the people into captivity in Babylon. The people of Judea were left behind, so after this time the Israelites were all referred to as Jews.

The story of Pesach

The story of Pesach begins when the ancestors of the Jewish people, the Hebrews, were slaves in ancient Egypt. God spoke to the prophet Moses and told him to go to the Pharaoh and ask the Pharaoh to let the Hebrew slaves go free.

Moses warned the Pharaoh that if he did not let the Hebrew slaves go free, God would bring disaster onto Egypt. The Pharaoh refused to listen to Moses, so God sent nine plagues to Egypt. But still the Pharaoh refused to let the Hebrew slaves go free.

Finally, God sent an angel to kill all the first born Egyptian children in each family.

So that the angel would know which people were the Hebrews, and not kill any of their children, God told Moses that all the Hebrew families should put lamb's blood on their doors. The angel would then know who was a Hebrew and 'pass over' those houses.

After this, the Pharaoh finally agreed to let the Hebrew slaves go free. They left Egypt in a great hurry, grabbing what they could and running out of their doors. But before they had gone far, the Pharaoh changed his mind and sent his army after them.

The Torah story teaches that when the Hebrews reached the Red Sea, God parted the waters so they could pass. The Egyptian army followed them. But once the Hebrews were safely across the sea, God closed the water up again and the Pharaoh's army was destroyed.

Weblink: www.CurriculumVisions.com

Celebrating Pesach

At the beginning of Pesach, a special meal called a seder is eaten at home. The seder includes readings and discussions, eating certain foods, singing songs, asking questions, and even playing games.

When the Hebrews left Egypt, they left in such a hurry that they did not have time to let their bread rise.

So, another way that people observe Pesach is by not eating any foods (such as bread and cakes) that contain yeast, which makes bread rise. Instead of these foods, a flat, unleavened bread, like a cracker, is eaten. This bread is called matzah.

The Pesach seder

Here are the parts of a Pesach seder. The seder is always done in this order. Any adult can lead the seder, and everyone participates.

1 A blessing is said

A cup of wine is poured for everyone (children can drink grape juice) and a blessing is said in honour of the holiday. Everyone drinks their cup of wine. Another cup of wine is poured into everyone's glass.

2 Washing

Everyone washes their hands.

3 Eating a green vegetable

Blessings are said and then everyone takes a piece of a green vegetable (usually parsley), dips it into salt water and eats it. The vegetable stands for the poverty of slavery; the salt water stands for the tears that are shed during slavery.

4 Breaking the matzah

The middle of the three matzahs on the table is broken into two pieces and one piece is hidden.

5 The Story of Pesach is told

Now the story of Pesach is read out loud. The story is written in a special book used during Pesach. Each person takes a turn to read. The first person to read is the youngest person at the table, who reads four questions about why Pesach night is different from other nights. The questions are answered by another person, usually an adult.

As the story of Pesach is read aloud, people may ask questions and discuss the answers. Everyone is encouraged to ask questions, to make sure they understand the meaning of the story.

During the telling of the story, the TEN PLAGUES of Egypt are discussed. Each person then uses a finger to take ten drops of wine out of their glass while the names of the plagues are recited.

At the end of the story, a blessing is said and everyone drinks their second cup of wine.

25

6 Washing

Everyone washes their hands a second time.

7 A prayer for grain

A blessing is said that thanks God for the gift of grain.

8 Eating matzah

A blessing is said that thanks God for matzah. Then everyone takes a small piece of matzah and eats it.

9 Eating bitter vegetables

A blessing is said over a bitter vegetable (called maror in Hebrew), such as horseradish, and everyone eats a piece. The bitter vegetable stands for the bitterness of slavery.

Then everyone takes a second piece of the bitter vegetable and dips it into haroset. This is a sweet mixture of fruits, nuts, spices and wine that stands for the mortar the Hebrews used when they worked as slaves in Egypt making buildings for the Pharaoh.

▼▶ On the table is a seder plate which contains the foods used in the seder. On the plate are: a hard-boiled egg, a roasted lamb shank bone, horseradish, parsley or celery greens, bitter herbs and haroset, a sweet paste made from fruit and nuts.

Everything on the plate has a special meaning. The shank bone stands for the burnt offerings made in the Temple in ancient times. The greens and the egg stand for new life and for spring. The horseradish and the bitter herbs stand for the bitterness of slavery. The haroset stands for the mortar that the Hebrews made when they worked as slaves.

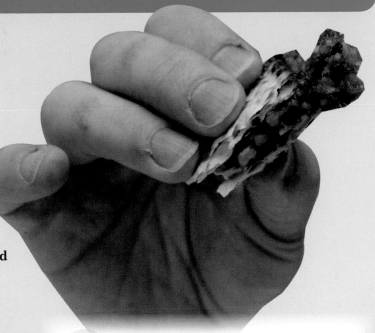

10 Making a matzah sandwich

Everyone makes themselves a small sandwich of matzah and bitter herbs and eats it. This is a tradition which began in medieval times.

▼ The meal traditionally begins by eating a hard-boiled egg. This stands for new life and for spring.

11 Eating dinner

Now, the main meal is eaten. This can be made of any foods, whatever each family likes. But remember that no leavening can be used, so there are no breads or foods made with yeast.

12 Searching for the hidden matzah

When everyone has finished eating, the children search for the piece of matzah that was hidden earlier. When it is found, everyone eats a piece.

13 Saying grace

After dinner a third cup of wine is poured for everyone, and everyone says grace. Then they drink the third cup of wine. A fourth cup of wine is poured for everyone.

An extra cup of wine is also poured in a special cup and left on the table. This is Elijah's cup. Elijah is an angel, and the wine is left in case Elijah decides to visit. The front door of the house is also opened for Elijah while blessings are said. At the end of the blessings, the door is closed again.

14 The last cup of wine

Several psalms are recited. A blessing is recited over the last cup of wine and everyone drinks.

Although this is the formal end of the seder, many families will continue to sing songs and talk for many more hours.

Purim

This holiday, on the 14th day of Adar, celebrates a time when a brave Jewish woman saved her people from death.

The story of Purim is told in the Torah Book of Esther. The heroes of the story are Esther and her cousin Mordecai, who raised her. The story takes place in the 5th century BCE. At this time, the kingdom of Babylon had conquered Israel and taken all the Jewish people of Israel to live in Persia.

One day, the king of Persia saw Esther and fell in love with her and decided to make her his queen. The king did not know that Esther was a Jew, because Mordecai told her not to reveal her identity.

Haman, an advisor to the king, hated Mordecai because Mordecai refused to bow down to Haman, so Haman plotted to destroy all the Jewish people. One day, Haman told the king, "There are people living in your kingdom who do not observe your laws and you should punish them." When he heard this, the king told Haman that he could punish these people any way he wished, and so Haman planned to kill all of the Jews.

Mordecai asked Esther to speak to the king and try to save the Jewish people. This was a dangerous thing for Esther to do, because anyone who came into the king's presence without being summoned could be put to death, and she had not been summoned. Esther fasted for three

▼ One Purim tradition is to eat filled pastries called hamentashen, or 'Haman's ears'. Synagogues hold fêtes and people wear fancy dress and throw things at pictures of Haman.

days to prepare then went to the king and told him of Haman's plot. The Jewish people were saved, and Haman was hanged on the gallows that had been prepared for Mordecai.

The word 'Purim' means 'lots' and refers to the lottery that Haman used to choose the date for the massacre.

Celebrating Purim

In the synagogue, the part of the Jewish Bible that tells the story of Esther is read out loud. Everyone dresses in costumes and hisses or boos whenever Haman's name is mentioned.

There may also be a parade and fair, and gifts of food are given to family members and to the poor.

Weblink: www.CurriculumVisions.com

Harvest celebrations

Jewish people also celebrate two important harvest festivals – a spring harvest and a summer harvest.

There are two important holy times that celebrate the harvest. They are called Sukkot and Shavuot.

Sukkot

The holiday of Sukkot begins five days after Yom Kippur and lasts for seven days. Sukkot actually celebrates two things. One is the spring harvest in ancient Israel. In the synagogue and at home special blessings and prayers are said while holding four types of plants that were important in ancient Israel. These are: a type of citrus fruit called an etrog, a date palm branch, a willow branch and a myrtle branch.

Sukkot also remembers an historical event. This is the time after the Hebrew people left Egypt, when they wandered in the desert for 40 years. During this time they were homeless and had to live in small huts, (the word sukkot means huts or booths).

▼ This boy is learning about Sukkot by drawing pictures of the plants that are used to celebrate the holiday.

◀▲ During Sukkot blessings are said while holding these plants.

▼ This is a model of a family eating a meal in their sukkot.

To remember this time, many Jewish families build a small hut outside their house. The family then eats their meals in the hut and may even sleep in it, weather permitting.

Shavuot

The other harvest festival is called Shavuot (Hebrew for weeks), or Pentecost. This holy day also celebrates two things. One is the summer harvest in ancient Israel, when there would be plenty of milk for the farmers. So, one Shavuot tradition is to eat dairy foods.

Shavuot also celebrates the time when God gave the Jewish Bible to the Hebrew people after they had left Egypt. This part of Shavuot is celebrated in the synagogue by reading the Torah story that tells about how God gave the Jewish holy books to Moses on Mount Sinai.

31

Weblink: www.CurriculumVisions.com

Index

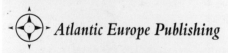

Curriculum Visions is a registered trademark of Atlantic Europe Publishing Company Ltd.

◆ *Atlantic Europe Publishing*

First published in 2007 by Atlantic Europe Publishing Company Ltd
Copyright © 2007 Earthscape

The right of Lisa Magloff to be identified as the author of this work has been asserted by her in accordance with the Copyright, Designs and Patents Act 1988.

Author
Lisa Magloff, MA

Religious Adviser
Nathan Abrams, PhD

Senior Designer
Adele Humphries, BA

Acknowledgements
The publishers would like to thank the following for their help and advice: Hendon Reform Synagogue, London; Bevis Marks Synagogue, London; Simon Marks school, London; the Bright family.

Photographs
The Earthscape Picture Library, except: (c=centre, t=top, b=bottom, l=left, r=right) pages 3, 4–5, 6, 8, 11b, 12–13, 14–15, 16–17, 18–19, 28 (inset) *ShutterStock*.

Illustrations
David Woodroffe

Designed and produced by
Earthscape

Printed in China by
WKT Company Ltd

Jewish holy days
– *Curriculum Visions*
A CIP record for this book is available from the British Library
ISBN: 978 1 86214 504 7

This product is manufactured from sustainable managed forests. For every tree cut down at least one more is planted.

Dedicated Web Site
There's more about other great Curriculum Visions packs and a wealth of supporting information on world religions and other subjects at our dedicated web site:
www.CurriculumVisions.com